Weirder and CUTER

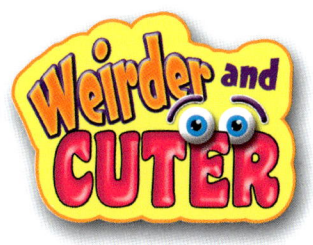

Platypus

by Jessica Rudolph

Consultant: Darin Collins, DVM
Director, Animal Health Programs
Woodland Park Zoo
Seattle, Washington

BEARPORT PUBLISHING
New York, New York

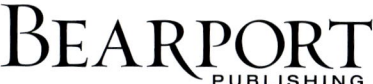

Credits

Cover, © Dave Watts/Alamy Stock Photo; TOC, © Dave Watts/Alamy Stock Photo; 4–5, © Dave Watts/Nature Picture Library; 6T, © Hans & Judy Beste/Ardea; 6B, © Iakov Filimonov/Shutterstock; 7, © D. Parer and E. Parer-Cook/Minden; 8–9, © Picassos/iStock; 9, © Dave Watts/Alamy Stock Photo; 10–11, © Dave Watts/Alamy Stock Photo; 11, © Auscape International Pty Ltd/Alamy Stock Photo; 12T, © National Geographic Creative/Alamy Stock Photo; 12BL, © D. Parer & E. Parer-Cook/Ardea; 12BR, © schankz/Shutterstock; 13, © D. Parer and E. Parer-Cook/Minden; 14, © Auscape/Ardea; 15, © blickwinkel/Alamy Stock Photo; 16T, © Guillem Lopez Borras/Shutterstock; 16BL, © Milosz Maslanka/Shutterstock; 16BR, © BMCL/Shutterstock; 17, © Dave Watts/Alamy Stock Photo; 18, © Matteo De Stefano/MUSE/cc by-sa 3.0; 18–19, © D. Parer and E. Parer-Cook/Minden; 20, © JASON EDWARDS/National Geographic Creative; 21, © Dave Watts/Minden; 22 (T to B), © LizCoughlan/Shutterstock, © Ronsmith/Shutterstock, © 2630ben/Shutterstock, and © andyschar/iStock; 23TL, © schankz/Shutterstock; 23TR, © National Geographic Creative/Alamy Stock Photo; 23BL, © D. Parer and E. Parer-Cook/Minden; 23BR, © Dave Watts/Alamy Stock Photo; Back Cover, © JohnCarnenolla/iStock.

Publisher: Kenn Goin
Editor: J. Clark
Creative Director: Spencer Brinker
Design: Debrah Kaiser

Library of Congress Cataloging-in-Publication Data

Names: Rudolph, Jessica, author.
Title: Platypus / by Jessica Rudolph.
Description: New York, New York : Bearport Publishing Company, Inc., [2018] | Series: Weirder and cuter | Audience: Ages 5–8. | Includes bibliographical references and index.
Identifiers: LCCN 2017002511 (print) | LCCN 2017004929 (ebook) | ISBN 9781684022649 (library) | ISBN 9781684023189 (ebook)
Subjects: LCSH: Platypus—Juvenile literature.
Classification: LCC QL737.M72 R83 2018 (print) | LCC QL737.M72 (ebook) | DDC 599.2/9—dc23
LC record available at https://lccn.loc.gov/2017002511

Copyright © 2018 Bearport Publishing Company, Inc. All rights reserved. No part of this publication may be reproduced in whole or in part, stored in any retrieval system, or transmitted in any form or by any means, electronic, mechanical, photocopying, recording, or otherwise, without written permission from the publisher.

For more information, write to Bearport Publishing Company, Inc., 45 West 21st Street, Suite 3B, New York, New York 10010. Printed in the United States of America.

10 9 8 7 6 5 4 3 2 1

Contents

Platypus	4
More Weird Mammals	22
Glossary	23
Index	24
Read More	24
Learn More Online	24
About the Author	24

What's this weird but cute **mammal**?

Long bill!

It's a platypus.

Furry body!

Big feet!

A platypus is very strange looking!

It has a wide, flat tail like a beaver.

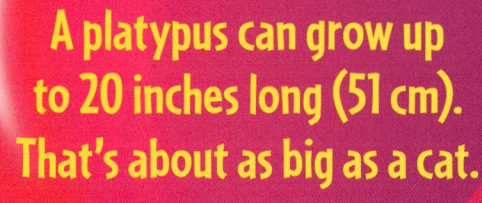

A platypus can grow up to 20 inches long (51 cm). That's about as big as a cat.

It also has a bill like a duck.

Yet the bill is soft and leathery.

bill

Platypuses live only in Australia.

They spend lots of time in lakes and rivers.

The platypus digs **burrows** near the water.

a platypus coming out of a burrow

Splash!

The little mammals are great swimmers.

They have webbed feet to paddle through the water.

They can steer with their tail!

webbed foot

The platypus comes to the surface every few minutes to take a breath of air.

Platypuses hunt for food in the water.

They search for tadpoles, crayfish, and worms.

The platypus moves its bill from side to side as it hunts.

All animals give off weak electrical signals.

The platypus's bill is very sensitive.

It can pick up electrical signals.

Look out!

Animals such as lizards, foxes, and pythons hunt platypuses.

Hiding underwater or in burrows helps the little creatures stay safe.

spur

The male platypus has **venomous** spurs on its back legs. It can use the spurs to fight off enemies.

In the spring, male and female platypuses **mate**.

After mating, the female digs a nesting burrow.

platypus eggs

Most mammals give birth to live young, but platypuses lay eggs!

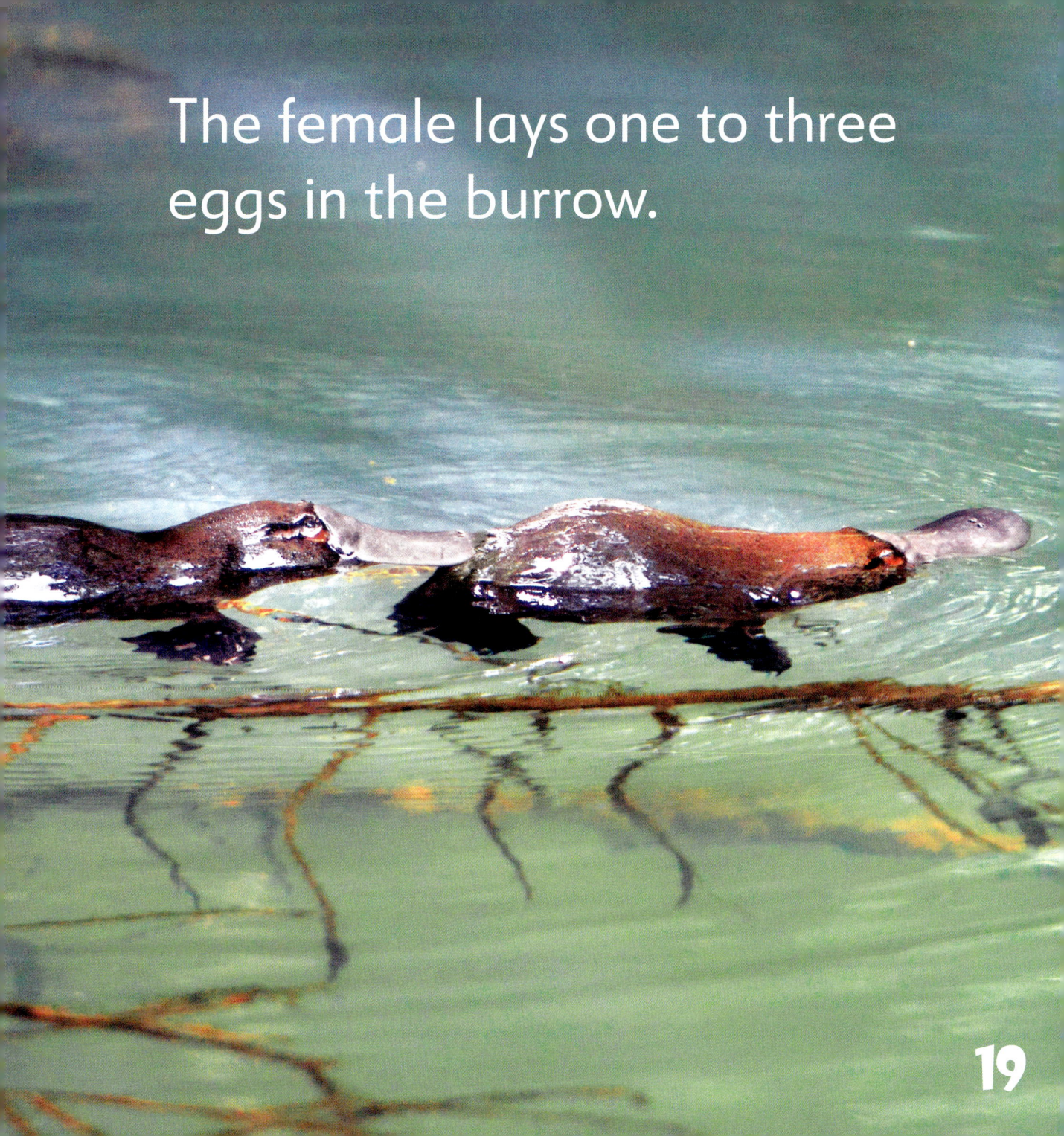

The female lays one to three eggs in the burrow.

About 12 days later, the babies hatch.

They drink their mother's milk.

The babies stay with their mother for about four months. Then they leave to live on their own.

More Weird Mammals

Echidna
Echidnas (eh-KID-nuhz) are also called spiny anteaters. Echidnas and platypuses are the only mammals that lay eggs!

Opossum
The female opossum carries her babies in a pouch, just like a kangaroo. When a large animal threatens an opossum, it pretends to be dead. This is called "playing possum."

Pangolin
The pangolin is the only mammal covered in scales. When an animal like a lion threatens it, the pangolin rolls up into a ball for protection.

Glossary

burrows (BUR-ohz) holes or tunnels dug in the ground by some animals for shelter

mammal (MAM-uhl) a warm-blooded animal that has hair or fur and drinks its mother's milk as a baby

mate (MAYT) to come together in order to have young

venomous (VEN-uhm-uhss) full of poison

Index

Australia 8
babies 20, 22
bill 4, 7, 14
burrows 9, 17, 18–19
eggs 18–19, 22
feet 5, 10–11
hunting 12–13, 14–15
mating 18–19
size 6
spurs 17
swimming 10–11
tail 6, 10

Read More

Collard, Sneed B., III. *A Platypus, Probably.* Watertown, MA: Charlesbridge (2005).

Whiting, Sue. *Platypus.* Somerville, MA: Candlewick (2016).

Learn More Online

To learn more about platypuses, visit
www.bearportpublishing.com/WeirderandCuter

About the Author

Jessica Rudolph lives in Connecticut. She has edited and written many books about history, science, and nature for children.